Valerie Schlitt
www.vsaprospecting.com

ISBN-13: 978-1477649305

ISBN-10: 1477649301

Printed in the USA

Table of Contents

1. Introduction: How to Build a Business Through Telephone Cold Calling

I was like most new business owners when I started my company. I had brand new letterhead, an idea, a logo, and just one customer.

I did not have a network to refer me business, nor did I have a website.

I remember thinking, "I'd better do something fast, or I will never get my business off the ground."

So, I started the old fashioned way. I got a calling list and a telephone. Then, I spent hours making lots and lots of telephone calls.

It worked!

Within months, I had clients across the country and two new assistants to help me with the work.

Since then, I have built an entire business making business to business (B2B) cold calls for other companies. This booklet will present all the basics to determine whether cold calling is for you and it will help you plan a successful campaign.

What this booklet will address:

1. Why firms avoid cold calling – and tools to put in place to overcome avoidance.

2. The immense benefits of B2B telephone cold calling.

3. Components critical to designing the right campaign.

4. Hiring an excellent cold calling team.

3

5. Writing a winning script.

6. Setting your expectations, and knowing what return to anticipate.

7. Answering the question of whether to create an internal operation or outsource your cold calling.

2. B2B Cold Calling: Perceived and Real Barriers to Success

Business to Business (B2B) cold calling is one of the most versatile and effective sources of acquiring prospective business clients, and can produce financial results for almost any firm.

Typically B2B cold calling is used to set appointments or drive prospects to a webinar. Many firms refer to it as "lead generation," "lead gen," or "appointment generation." But the entire process starts with the basic cold call.

Before you go ahead and launch a cold calling program, however, consider these perceived and real barriers to success.

Perceived Barriers
#1: Cold calling is just like consumer telemarketing. Equating B2B cold calling with consumer telemarketing, many managers and cold callers themselves project their own feelings onto their prospects. Their dislike and fear of interrupting or annoying prospects overwhelms them.

Let me tell you, if you truly believe your calls are negative interruptions, you will never be successful. Your callers will not have confidence and your prospects will not respect them.

I personally regard cold calling as an opportunity to present information to individuals who otherwise would not have access to it, and to provide real solutions to actual business challenges. That's the belief system successful callers have when they make cold calls. Prospects can hear it in their voices and respond positively.

#2: Cold calling is too expensive. Many people new to cold calling are startled by its expense. Yes, cold calling is labor

intensive, making it more costly than an advertisement in a local paper. However, cold calling can be far more effective than a single advertisement. It's the return on investment that must be considered, not just the cost.

More importantly, cold calling is absolutely affordable to most firms on a pilot (trial) basis. The pilot will help you learn whether you have the potential to succeed in the future – and whether you would be wise to make the investment.

Real Barriers
#1: As with all marketing campaigns, cold calling also requires an appetite for risk. You will not know in the beginning whether your cold calling program will be successful.

#2: Even when cold calling programs are successful, the results are inconsistent. Firms who succeed using cold calling generally make long-term commitments and view results over extended time periods.

#3: Lastly, prospects who originate through cold calling typically require a great deal of cultivation by skilled sales people. Do not mistake them for warm leads.

In short, successful cold calling requires a long term view and financial investment, a willingness to take risks, and strong sales skills to close leads.

If your firm can make these commitments, cold calling may be one of your best sources to uncover "hard to find" prospects. It may be your biggest competitive advantage and a source of sustainable revenue and client growth.

I have seen companies earn returns on their cold calling efforts multiple times their initial investments. You may be able to do so too.

3. The Benefits: What Makes Cold Calling Unique?

Cold calling is an amazing way to expand your reach into new industries, new geographies, even to new departments within existing clients' firms. Cold calling enables you to find and talk to decision makers directly! It's not passive. You don't need to wait until decision makers notice you. You find them.

You can focus your investment on those with the highest likelihood to purchase your products or services. Unlike billboards, internet banner ads, or print advertising, you won't waste money on decision makers who are absolutely outside your target market.

Importantly, cold calling allows you to reach decision makers who may be on the verge of making a decision BEFORE they call your competitors.

You can also use telephone calls to connect with individuals who attended your presentation; potentially these individuals wanted to connect with you, but once they returned to the office they faced far more pressing demands.

There is no other marketing tool that is as flexible in personalizing messages, in allowing you to start and stop at will, and in opening doors to new opportunities. You can stay in touch with decision makers who are not yet ready to purchase, so you are the one they choose when they are prepared to buy.

Cold calling is interactive. You can learn the reasons why decision makers won't buy. Then, you can immediately tailor your message to address these concerns. I hear all the time about firms who have never cold called, who have built their entire businesses through referrals. To these firms, I say, "How much bigger could your business be if you implemented a cold calling program!?"

4. Key Success Criteria for B2B Telephone Cold Calling Programs.

Once you are committed to implementing a successful cold calling campaign, you are ready to begin preparing for the program. Preparation is absolutely critical in creating a successful campaign.

Here are the four most critical elements to plan.

#1 A Good Calling List: Firms on your list must mirror your client base.

The list contributes 60% - 70% towards the campaign's success so it is the single most critical component to your cold calling program. The best way to select the list is to look at your current customers.

- The firms you are calling must resemble very closely the kinds of companies who purchase your product/service, and have a high likelihood of needing a service such as yours at some point in the companies' life cycle.
- Typically, the selection criteria include: industry, geographic area, employee size, revenue size, and length in business. There are many other criteria as well.
- As a rule of thumb, if 50% of the firms on your list are not within your target market, you should not continue calling. You will waste time and money.

Note: There are many sources of lists, including: FJ Associates, 914-320-9785; Infogroup, 888-808-0047; Dun and Bradstreet, 610-882-7505; Hoover's, Inc. 812-374-4592

#2 A Compelling Message: Your script must be understandable in 10 – 15 seconds.

When you cold call decision makers at the workplace, you are their last priority. Your call is totally unexpected and potentially unwanted.   Therefore, your message must be

engaging and compelling. (See Ingredients of a Good Script, below.)

- Make your message short: 10 – 15 seconds is all the time you have to capture the decision maker's attention.
- Communicate only one concept. Asking a prospect to think and make too many decisions is asking too much.
- Talk about benefits not features – always remember prospects want to hear "what's in it for me."
- Make sure you are very specific about what you want your prospect to do next and ask for it.

Note: Professionals who specialize in effective script writing include: Scott Channell, 978-927-5099; Cathy Edwards, 864-676-1577

#3 An Intriguing Offer: Create a sense of urgency or a special reason to take action.

Wherever possible, try to sweeten your request with something attractive for the prospect – something that will help him want to say "yes."

Remember, your goal is to sell the appointment, not the product or service. Whatever your offer is, it must be designed to help gain agreement to a meeting.

- If you are selling websites, your offer might be a free assessment of the company's website.
- Watch out: the offer must not cheapen your service or make you look desperate. For example, do not offer a year's worth of cleaning services at 50% off.
- For some products or services, there is simply no appropriate offer. It is fine in these cases to not include an offer; just be aware that an offer could enhance your results.

#4 Quality Callers: Your team must sound knowledgeable and credible.

The caller's tone must essentially invite the prospect into a conversation, and avoid anything that might distract focus from the key message. (See Profile of an Excellent Cold Caller, below.)

- Decision makers must believe they are talking to a trusted representative of the company.
- In no cases should the decision maker believe that the caller is filling a part-time "telemarketing" job.
- The caller's tone must be business-like, slightly animated, engaging and void of all hesitation.
- Your calling team must quickly internalize the key points in the script and begin to convey these points in their own words, without reading the script.
- The delivery can never get in the way of the message; hence the caller's diction must be easily understood and pleasing to hear. We recommend avoiding incorrect grammar, strong accents, or mispronounced words.

Note: Any firm that performs pre-employment behavioral testing would be a great resource to assess caller potential. Also, using role playing during the interview process can predict effectiveness. Once hired, a caller can demonstrate whether he/she is a good fit within two to three weeks.

5. Profile of an Excellent Cold Caller

Because your calling team is so important to the success of your campaign, you will need to identify callers with the right personalities.

A great cold caller is really hard to find. When hiring callers, you cannot simply pull someone from a customer service role or an administrative role and expect them to be successful on the phones. Most of the qualities that make a cold caller excellent are inherent in his or her basic personality.

An excellent cold caller's personality is almost an oxymoron. He or she must possess a fantastic combination of tolerance, perseverance and tenacity PLUS have the ability to be assertive, proactive and engaging.

A great cold caller is also intuitive. The caller hears the slightest hesitation in the prospect's voice and is able to ask the right question to keep the conversation going.

Let's take two examples:

- Sally is making outbound calls for a building maintenance service. She begins talking to a prospect and is creating camaraderie. The prospect says he doesn't need her service. Then, out of the blue, the prospect announces, "but I have another location that might be in need." Sally probes about the other location and sets up a sales appointment.

  At first glance, this doesn't seem particularly special. But, a cold caller with fewer capabilities would not have been so tenacious. She would have stopped the conversation as soon as the prospect said he had no need. She would not have engaged the prospect in conversation – and would never have learned about the second location.

Talking to a less engaging caller, the prospect's reaction would probably have been "I've got to get off this phone." Instead, Sally made talking easy and fun because she built camaraderie and asked questions. Just the few extra seconds on the phone changed this prospect from a flat "no" to a viable opportunity.

- Jenny has been calling prospects for hours and has rarely spoken to a decision maker. This is typical for the industry Jenny is targeting, but she knows one lead is worth a great deal of money.

  This is Jenny's third time calling the same list of senior-level executives. This is the worst situation to be in for a cold caller. If callers do not speak to prospects, they get no practice internalizing the message and making the words their own.

  Jenny knows that although she has spoken to no one, she must appear totally relaxed when a decision maker eventually picks up the phone.

  Jenny is determined. All of a sudden a C-level executive answers his phone. Jenny begins a conversation. A moment ago she was feeling desperate and defeated because she had not been able to reach anyone. Now, she is upbeat, positive and confident. To Jenny's delight, the prospect decides to listen further, asks questions and Jenny is able to set a phone appointment for tomorrow.

Cold callers with less experience would not have been able to move as quickly from "perseverance mode" into "conversation mode" as Sally and Jenny. The positive attitude, confidence and intuition that both Sally and Jenny possess helped greatly.

As noted above, the quality of the caller is just one ingredient to a successful cold calling campaign, far below the quality of

the list. But if you don't have a solid calling team you will never fully optimize results.

6. Ingredients of a Compelling Script

A cold caller should always sound natural and never memorize or read a script.

However, every cold caller should have a simple sheet of paper, or a computer screen, that contains the key points of the message/script.

A good script or message includes four sections, which must take no longer than 10 – 15 seconds to communicate:

1)   Introduction: Your name and the company's name and what you do.
2)   Benefits to the prospect: A sentence or two, if needed, about your product or service and how it helps prospects. If possible, use this sentence to differentiate your product from a competitor.
3)   Credibility builder: A statement about the market you serve and/or the clients you work with. This establishes your firm as legitimate.
4)   A call to action with an offer, when possible: A statement that summarizes why you are calling. You want to set a time to meet, a meeting over the phone, or permission to send information. The offer is used to increase the prospect's likelihood of saying "yes."

The above points are required to start a conversation with prospects that have interest. That's all.

When a prospect responds "no"; the caller should ask one or two probing questions and repeat the call to action – a request for a meeting, for example. If the prospect again says "no," the caller must quickly move to the next record and start all over again. In B2B cold calling, do not invest more than two minutes overcoming objections, and do not try to convince prospects to change their minds. This is a waste of time and money.

 14

For prospects who have some level of interest, but haven't yet said "yes," cold callers need back-up material including questions to ask. The script should contain 1) additional benefits of their products/ services; 2) names of companies with whom their company works; 3) probing questions to ask; 4) a brief history of their company; 5) a tiny bit of information about the product features; and 6) a call-back number.

The hardest and most essential part of the script for the callers to say consistently is the "call to action," that is, the request for a meeting or a webinar. Callers who anticipate a negative response will want to avoid this part of the message. I cannot stress the importance of consistently stating the "call to action." In fact, I can virtually guarantee that your results will be 15% - 20% higher if your callers ask for the appointment on every call.

Here are two sample scripts. Notice how both introduce the firm, provide minimal, but credible information about how they help clients, and ask for the close.

Sample Script for an Accounting Consultancy:

> Hello, this is _____ calling from ABC Group, a boutique finance and accounting consultancy.
>
> As consultants, we handle a variety of demanding accounting issues for small to middle market public companies – helping solve last minute surprises and anticipate future issues from 10-K and 10Q filings to extremely complex transactions.
>
> **[First attempt to close]** Our founding partner would like the opportunity to meet with you to introduce our firm for any immediate needs or just to bounce some ideas for the future. No obligation. Can we set a date and time that fits your schedule?

<u>Sample Script for a Software Provider to Auto Manufacturers:</u>

Hello _____ my name _____. I work for XYZ Company.

Are you familiar with us? We provide software exclusively for the auto industry. I'm wondering how you use software in your business. Do you have an order entry system? (Use the additional questions if the prospect has not yet engaged in conversation: Do you have a production system? How is it working out for you?)
Are you interested in scheduling a call in the next couple of weeks where we could discuss whether we would be a good fit?

Author's notes:

1) Never start a conversation with "Hi, how are you?" This is a dead give-away that you are a sales person. Plus it gives the prospect a second or two to create an excuse to leave the conversation.
2) Writing scripts is hard. The script writer must consistently have the prospect in mind. Often, I find that companies want to include a myriad of points in the script that address their products' enhanced features. In the introductory portion of the script, the prospect only cares about "what's in it for me." Being long-winded only makes scripts less compelling and interesting.

7. What Results Can You Expect from Cold Calling?

Every cold calling campaign is different. Results vary hugely by industry, target market, time of year, offer, and desired outcome, among other factors. Even the same campaign implemented in a slightly different geographic area will have different results.

Successful cold calling programs should aim to produce financial results within five months, and generate a return of five to eight times the cold calling investment.

Here are some guidelines of what you can expect.

Appointments:

- One to three appointments per hour for low cost products where usage is high, risk of setting the appointment is low, and there are no entrenched incumbents. Water and Coffee Delivery and Printing Services are two examples.

- One to two appointments per 20 – 40 hours for complex, high ticket products where incumbents have long contracts and there are barriers to switching. CPA Services and Medical Billing Services are examples.

Decision Makers:

- Five to eight conversations with decision makers every 10 hours when targeting C-level executives.

- Three to ten conversations with decision makers per hour when targeting plant managers, administrative assistants, and junior level managers.

Calls per Hour

- 8 to 15 calls per hour when calling large companies when you do not have a decision maker name.

- 15 to 20 calls per hour when calling smaller companies or firms where you have direct dial numbers and a decision maker name.

8. Wait, There Are Four More Success Criteria!

In addition to the four most critical elements discussed above, there are a host of other important components to a cold calling program. I have provided just a few below.

#5 Sufficient Time: Give the program enough time to prove its success.

Many firms have the notion that cold calling will be immediately successful. They believe that everyone who answers the phone will want their product/service. This is rarely the case. Give your program at least 150 – 250 hours of calling time before declaring it a success or failure. Think of it this way. This time period is equivalent to only one month or one and a half months of a sales person's full time work on your program.

#6 Metrics: Measure, measure, measure.

As mentioned in a previous chapter, there are several key metrics that most sophisticated telemarketing programs measure.

If you know that you need one appointment every five hours, and your program is producing one appointment every three hours, you will need to determine how to increase your appointment rate.

If you do not measure your results, you will not know whether you are on track. You will also not know what behaviors you need to change in order to improve results.

7 Supervision: Ensure callers have the help they need to succeed.

I recommend "management by walking around," as well as giving callers immediate feedback and the ability to ask

questions. When supervising the cold calling team, ensure the manager maintains a positive environment and keeps the callers motivated. Callers receive enough rejection on the phone; they will not be productive if they receive too much negative reinforcement from managers.

#8 Program Design: Test approaches to define the prospecting process that works.

You'll need to make many decisions about leaving voice messages, the number of calls to make to each decision maker, and whether to send more information, and more.

There are absolutely no rules that apply across programs regarding these decisions. Successful cold calling programs test and see what works best. They modify and improve.

In general:
1) Leaving voicemails only works if you have a highly targeted list and a highly desired product. Your voice message must be 10 seconds or shorter. If you get no return calls after one week of leaving messages, stop leaving voicemails.
2) Sending more information is not wise, unless you have qualified your prospects and they agree to specific dates and times for follow-up calls after receiving the information.
3) Making three to four attempts to reach each prospective decision maker is effective because individuals are rarely at their desks. Typically, scheduling these calls two to three days apart has the best results.

My recommendations above are general approaches, but I have seen highly successful programs that do not follow these approaches at all. Again, testing and learning is a critical component to identifying the optimal program design.

9. Whether to Outsource or Set-up In-house Cold Calling

A big question for many firms is whether to establish an internal cold calling operation or whether to hire an outsourced firm to make the calls.

There is no easy answer. This is as simple as I can put it. Building a cold calling capability within a firm whose main mission is not telephone prospecting is incredibly challenging.

Hiring the right people, installing the right phone system and choosing the right customer relationship management (CRM) software (to name just a few required activities) all demand a focus on this unit that your company may or may not want to apply.

Often the expense is identical if you house the cold calling effort internally or if you outsource the work.

When you outsource to a trusted firm, you can turn on and off the pace of calling as needed. You don't need to worry about finding extra qualified resources or laying people off when you ramp up or slow down. However, if you do decide to outsource, you must feel comfortable with your cold calling partner.

Make sure you get references and do not get locked into a long-term contract. I recommend starting with a pilot program of at most 100 hours.

There are two cases where I would highly recommend using internal staff:

#1: Staff Availability If you have excellent staff who are not otherwise occupied and they can focus on cold calling. They must have the right skill sets and someone to supervise them.

#2: Mission Critical Activity If the cold calling process is a proprietary part of your business, and you don't want to risk competitors learning how you target new businesses, identify leads and bring them to the next level in the sales process. In this case, cold calling is one of your mission-critical processes and can remain internal.

For advice on whether to outsource, call me at 856-240-8100, Steve Fagan at 856-340-3868 or Andrew Pauson at 215-657-4281.

10. A Case Story: What it looks like in real life...

Here is a case story about Legal Social Media, Inc. a firm that writes Facebook entries, blogs and tweets for personal injury law firms.

This is a cutting edge service offered by a small, yet successful firm. The company had always gotten clients through word of mouth, and decided to broaden its reach by using outbound cold callers.

Legal Social Media was new to outbound B2B cold calling. This is how the firm structured the campaign:

1) The list: The firm ordered a list of small personal injury law firms, with practices comprised of 2 – 3 attorneys.
2) The message: Legal Social Media used a fairly compelling message, essentially: you need to use social media to get your next clients, or your competitors will get them first.
3) The offer: The firm chose not to include a special offer, such as "first month free," or "first twitter account free for every Facebook account."
4) The callers: The calling team was competent and had experience targeting attorneys.

The campaign's primary objective was to set telephone appointments. The second objective was to send emails to interested firms with the goal of making a telephone follow-up to set a time to talk.

In the first 25 hours, Legal Social Media set 1 telephone appointment which did not result in a sale. The firm also sent 12 emails to law offices, but could not reach the attorney decision makers after sending the emails in the short remaining time.

After these 25 hours, Legal Social Media decided to stop the program. The company concluded they would not produce a sufficiently high ROI, based on these early results.

So, what happened? Was Legal Social Media right to stop the program? Here is my analysis of the campaign:

1) Regarding the calling list, it turns out that the decision makers were the attorneys themselves. Talking directly to attorneys requires multiple phone calls, and thus meant Legal Social Media would need to spend more time and money than budgeted.
2) The message was fairly compelling, but just not strong enough. This is a cutting edge service and attorneys are slow to adopt new products and services.
3) The lack of an offer hurt. Perhaps if there had been a special offer to sway a few more decision makers into scheduling a telephone meeting, more attorneys may have stopped to listen. Without an offer, and with already busy schedules, attorneys didn't see a reason to stop their existing work and act now.
4) The outbound callers were clear, confident and friendly. Unfortunately, they rarely spoke to decision makers or key influencers.

This case study is a classic example of a well-planned program that had most of the right ingredients, but overlooked critical factors. In the end, the biggest factor was the low frequency of reaching the attorneys directly and the lack of urgency on attorneys' part to respond to information sent.

Perhaps if Legal Social Media had the budget to continue the program longer term, had created an effective process for converting information seekers into sales potentially used an introductory offer, this program could have proven successful and resulted in a positive ROI.

However, Legal Social Media's budget could not support a longer term campaign. Continuing this program was unsustainable for the small firm; but the fact that this company tried the campaign and learned from it will position Legal Social Media well when it implements similar future campaigns.

I purposefully used this case study to show how the two barriers introduced in Chapter 1, the willingness to make a long term investment and having strong sales skills, can prevent a potentially successful program from achieving full potential.

11. Summary

1. Cold calling is one of the most versatile and effective sources of finding prospective customers, and can produce a strong return on investment for almost any firm.
2. To be successful, however, management and callers must consider cold calls as opportunities to provide real solutions to actual business challenges.
3. Firms with the most effective cold calling programs make long term financial investments and possess strong sales skills. If your firm cannot commit to these, cold calling is not for you.
4. The four most critical components for a successful cold calling campaign include: the list, the message, the offer and quality callers. Obviously, there are other factors, but these are the most essential.
5. The list is the single highest influencer of success and contributes 60 – 70% towards the program's effectiveness.
6. At the same time, if your firm does not have a solid calling team, it will never fully optimize results.
7. Asking for the "close" (an appointment, a webinar, etc.) on every single call, can virtually guarantee a 15% - 20% increase in results.
8. Every cold calling campaign is different and results vary hugely by industry, geography and time of year, among other factors. However, a successful cold calling program should aim to produce financial results twice to five times the amount of the cold calling investment.
9. There are two cases where investing in an internal cold calling operation makes optimal sense: 1) You have excellent and available staff; 2) Your prospecting process is highly confidential and differentiates you from competitors.
10. Many firms who have never cold called brag about having built their entire businesses through referrals. To these firms, I say, "How much bigger could your businesses be if you would implement a cold calling program!?"

About the Author

Valerie earned her BA from the University of Pennsylvania and her MBA from the Wharton School. Formerly a consultant with KPMG Consulting and Pricewaterhouse-Coopers Consulting, Valerie started her career in marketing management positions at American Express, Travelers and CIGNA. Valerie's focus area is in direct marketing including call centers' roles to support marketing campaigns, direct response ads and strategy development. Valerie founded Valerie Schlitt Associates, Inc. in 2001 and brings her bottom-line focus to the firm, where the goal is to achieve financial results for clients.

www.ingramcontent.com/pod-product-compliance
Lightning Source LLC
Chambersburg PA
CBHW072030190526
45166CB00015B/1778